# This Skin I'm in

Ebony Gilbert

blood
moon
POETRY

This Skin I'm In

Cover art by Abbie Laura Smith
ISBN: 978-1-7399155-1-3
Imprint: blood moon POETRY

There are so many beautiful people who make up my universe.
You know who you are.

This book is dedicated to Steve, Jordana and my Mum;
my sun, my moon and my stars.

This Skin I'm In

# Note from the Editor:

When we first decided to move into print, it was Ebony's poetry I could see on the page. A punch to the gut, her work sits in the pit of my stomach a long time after reading. That's just how she writes. Everything out, nothing left in. You feel her words: they reverberate through your bones and end up jangling just behind your heart.

Right now, it feels like we're living in a world where anything can happen TO women, but we are nowhere near tangible change FOR women. Yet at blood moon we have seen an increase in submissions and subscribers. Women want to write for us and write beside us. While we're not seeing enough action, I am starting to read more words. Poems, articles, books, blog posts. The women are writing.

This Skin I'm In could be a manifesto for our time. Ebony writes about the universal female experience, unifying us with her songs of shame, survival, rebirth and profound strength. Her vulnerability is a visceral reminder that to grow is to lay bare what you are told to hide. I felt a shift within as I reached the end of the book and the sizzle crack of excitement that comes when, as an Editor, you know you're about to publish something really special.

What I hope you find here is a reminder that you are not alone. As women we may be facing some of the most challenging and dangerous times of our lives, but we are also more united than ever in our determination not to be cowed. No more bowing out. We stand together. So lift your heads and hearts, raise your banners and sing out the words you find here – "I survived".

And know that more words are coming. The women are writing, and blood moon POETRY are going to be printing what they have to say.

Lunar love,

Holly Ruskin
Editor-in-chief & co-founder
blood moon POETRY
www.bloodmoonpoetry.com

# Note from the Author:

A year ago I began sharing my poetry, despite every part of every one of my selves screaming to stay silent.

This Skin I'm In is a vulnerable exploration of living in a body (my body) through trauma and the profoundly unjust shame, addiction and life-saving yet debilitating dissociation that accompany it.

I'll admit it feels like I'm doing a full frontal, which deeply unnerves me but also seems a natural progression in unveiling and disposing of a bit more of this shame illusion. The process has felt like a dangerous excavation at times and only occasionally I've remembered that when we dig out old foundations, we create a pool into which we can allow the pouring of light.

I have procrastinated on this as a means of self-protection. That's the thing with this stuff though isn't it? The shame wants to keep it a secret for fear of being abandoned, judged or of making our loved ones feel bad. I'm so thankful that the higher plan put Holly from blood moon POETRY in my path who asked me to share my work with you. I am also grateful to have so many good people in my life who love and listen and support in their own unique ways.

Composing these pieces has been a kind of coalescence; a merging of the inner and outer worlds, so that they might meet each other at first with an awkward glance and perhaps later with a tentative holding of hands. The poems seek to hold a microphone up to every organ and bone and the skin they're in and let them speak their version of events. They are a declaration of tenacity and of victory. They are an apology to me. And they are a carrier pigeon to survivors: do what you need to do to get through. That could be therapy, medication, sobriety or all of the above. But it could also look like smoking, cutting, drinking or overeating some days and those behaviours ARE you trying to take care of yourself. They may not be considered healthy but are sometimes all we can do to survive another day, until we can claw our way to shore and ask for help. The moon is out there even on the darkest, cruellest days.

And however you're coping today is okay. You are okay. Most important-ly, you don't have to do it alone.

Finally, this book is a dedication -

To my thirty-nine-year-old self who wears all her stories.

To my early thirties self who soberly grieved the many shocking diagno-ses after the birth of her son.

To the sister who lost her brother.

To my early twenties self who braved sobriety and much more. To my earlier twenties self who drank and drugged to numb it all. To teenage me who wore spice lipliner and made herself throw up every day.

And to little me. The bravest, most beautiful girl I have ever known. I love you. I hear you. I'm here.

P.s.: When the super-talented Abbie was designing the cover, she asked if I wanted her to model the torso on my own body, to which I immedi-ately shouted, "no!!!". I still struggle to accept my body. I don't even like to wear short-sleeved tops. Two days later, in a moment of boldness and my usual impulsivity, I wrote her and our wonderful, gracious Editor Holly an email which went like this:

Dear Holly & Abbie,
I've changed my mind. Here are some naked selfies of me. This book is about ME and MY body, so here I am. No filters. FUCK YOU SHAME!

Love,

Ebony x

# Contents

This Skin I'm In

# Foreword

Being vulnerable is an art form. It's equal measures of sincerity, openness, shame, and confidence - and This Skin I'm In embraces every part of what it means to be vulnerable. Ebony leaves everything on the table, or page in this case, and lets us in on the nuances of being a survivor. We hear from her body parts in 'Suits', as if animated with their own thoughts, we hear from her throughout her lifetime, the innocence of her teens in 'A Minor' and the search to try and get that back in 'Morning has broken'. We hear from her self-doubt, how it cuts her down and then how she cuts it down, ending her collection with the powerful words: 'If only you knew how exquisite you really are. I will stitch you back together. I will mend you.'

Ebony began to share her poetry only twelve months ago, but this debut collection feels like a lifetime of work - because it is. Every piece feels like a time capsule of emotion, locked in and left in its most raw state. What a talent it is, to tap into yourself throughout the years, when most of us bury our past incarnations.

Poetry, to me, isn't about the forms it takes - we've moved beyond needing poets to form perfect sonnets, or who know the difference between a Ghazal and a Pantoumn - it's about what you say. It's about committing and creating. Ebony commits, there's no trepidation or one toe in the water, she's metaphorically streaking. I can't wait to share this collection with the survivors in my life, it's a hand-squeeze of a book - it's saying 'hey, I've been there too.'

There's a line in Suits, that will stay with you forever: 'You ever feel like you want to take your skin off? Like, all of it?'

**Chloe Grace Laws**
Founder @fgrlsclub
Follow Me @chloegracelaws
Glamour Magazine Social Media Director

This Skin I'm In

# My graffiti heart

Me and my body
got a divorce,
I cheated on her
with no remorse,
kicked her
while she was on all fours.
No conversation,
no "I think we should separate",
just painted over her,
decided to redecorate.
Three gloss layers
and a top-coat,
melted her into the concrete,
never even left a note.
Brand new canvas
splashed with yellow,
danced about
all night to techno,
fell over in drunk stilettos,
strings of strange bedfellows.

The thing is though
I miss her.
All that realness
sketched and smeared,
the unspoken words
illicitly sprayed
beneath the veneer.
I miss
the exposed brick
so thick
only a sledgehammer
could be enough
to even scuff
the surface,
strip back the hurt,

13

chip my apology
into the dirt.

Would you consider
getting back together?
Would you ever?

She scribbles on a postcard,
'But you broke
my art.
It's just so long we've been apart.'

I'll keep trying.
Text her,
send her flowers,
try to mend
her graffiti heart.
Send her love letters,
earn her trust,
put in the hours,
stroke her back,
play her
the Edward Scissorhands soundtrack.

Come on legs.
I want you back

This Skin I'm In

This Skin I'm In

# A Minor

She swallows some soap.
The water trickles down her thighs
leaving a trail of something
behind.
She doesn't know it yet,
but it will stay her whole lifetime
like a thumbprint in her mind.

She stands in front of the mirror.
Traces fingertips,
ten waning half moons
over some lips
that somehow look a different shape,
like they've been plucked from her face
and stuck
onto an unknown landscape.

A silent howl.
Vocal chords strung taut,
abandoned cello housed within the throat
she thought
belonged to her.
The girl in the mirror sings
F so sharp
her strings carve the air in two;
before and after.

She wills her hips to move.
To walk downstairs
to dinner and laughter.
Prays for the standing-on-end hairs
on her arms
to flatten themselves,
her hindbrain to feign a normal
that will never exist again.

She didn't see him.
But she smelt him and she felt him.

This Skin I'm In

# Unalone

Daydream doodles,
his name scratched
onto your arm with a compass,
diet noodles for lunch and dinner,
your lovely young face
looking thinner.
The first break,
not your arm but your heart.
I'll make you a cast,
draw love hearts on it,
this pain won't last.
Oh baby,
downing Southern Comfort
won't mend the hurt.
Let me hold you,
wash that school shirt
worn loose like your confidence,
tucked into your rolled-up skirt.
Eyebrows as plucked
as the strings of your beautiful heart.
Fourteen was the worst.
My lips pursed,
powerless,
you run down the street where he lived,
where you first kissed,
tears wetting your girlish cheeks,
Never Ever on repeat.
You always thought he'd cheat.
Okay, sink half a snakebite and black
just don't take him back.
I'll save you twos,
walk with you down The Avenues,
get you some new shoes.
"Please don't leave me" you whisper.
And I stroke your skinny arms
from shoulders to palms.

Never ever.

This Skin I'm In

# Chalk mark

I ran so fast
I left myself behind,
a trail of damage in my wake,
that ache,
looking for something bigger.
A mummy-shaped hole and
lipstick so thick and
skin so thin
and consciousness opaque.
The shame made her feel so unpretty
in that seedy city
and the young woman began to evaporate.
Heart-shaped loneliness,
eyes with no shine,
left her value on the District line.

This Skin I'm In

# Text me when you get home

Don't walk alone
Ear to phone
Thumb over the 9
Breath misting the air with
Sparkling wine
Walk in a straight line
Not that way
That alleyway
It's not well lit
Sweat collects in armpits
Fear moonlit
Shoulders back girl
Bold as brass
Through the underpass
Across the car park
Eyes scan the dark
Key chain macraméd
Around knuckles
Strike points memorised
Take him by surprise
Kick to the groin
Knees buckle
Snap fingers at the joints
Thumbs in the eyes
Get him lengthwise
Use your knees
Remember your keys
Catch the last bus home
Coat pulled tight
How is it okay
That this is a normal Friday night?

This Skin I'm In

# Morning has broken

Got my first pill
Danced with that guy
From the Streets
Dressed as a bunny girl
Champagne and beats
Tuesday nights
Rolled up receipts
Flashing lights
Backseats
Laddered tights
Hotel suites
Whisky chasers
All the faces
Smashed chandeliers
Trippin' on my laces
Pulse races
Kissing the girls
Kissing the boys
Writhing in
The noise
Ears destroyed
Thumping floors
Hammering heart
Jaw swinging
Mouth minging
Just another
Wednesday morning
Curtains drawn
Chorus dawning
Some guy snoring
Time for mourning

This Skin I'm In

# It's Tiffany

Maybe if I'd grown up
in a tower block
or I had cuff links
and a cock,
they would have kept their
hands in their pockets
with their wallets
and Tiffany lockets
to seduce the one with the shy smile,
pass her around,
be nice for a while,
get her immobile.
I could use artistic license
and describe them
as flabby or scabby
but they weren't.
They were clean-cut,
beautiful and athletic,
arms with walnut skin,
strong enough to pin
a pretty dumb girl down,
make her feel pathetic,
flaunt her around
on a night on the town,
soho triple vodkas downed.
It was bound
to end with
tearstained cheeks
and mascara streaks.
I pick up my bag.
Never again.
At least not until next week.

This Skin I'm In

# When I'm gone

Push through,
Push forward,
Do it til it hurts,
Screaming for your mama
On your knees in the dirt.
Pass out,
Up again,
Left arm hanging off.
I'm okay,
I smile and say,
Just need a bit more hairspray.
Soul for sale
I advertise,
Crossing boundary lines,
Skipping over the membrane
Thin as newborn skin
Between out there
And this body I'm in.
Ankle sprained,
Heels bloodstained,
Bright lights,
Carnage,
Face to pavement
Swept up with garbage,
Don't know what's going on.
Then everything turns black
And I'm gone.

This Skin I'm In

# Bring me home

Eyelids closed
like petals at night,
violets
in the dying light.
Undressed,
laying to rest
in the afterglow,
the slow blow
to the hollow
where my collarbones
meet and moan
for that unknown thing
to bring me home
into my body.

This Skin I'm In

# Get your coat

I woke in tears.
Had it actually happened?
Anesthetic wearing thin.
Handbag on the side,
bruises blackened,
the coat I'd been wearing.

This Skin I'm In

# Thief

Too much cold space around my body,
suspended in midair.
My warm breath
mists the room
where my bed is
and hot tears slide down my throat.
Irresistible and devastating and deep,
grief pads gently through my mind,
the only friend I want to keep.
She slowly seeps
into my bones,
and this quiet grief,
this exquisite grief,
this thief
is here to stay.

This Skin I'm In

# Suits

You ever feel like you want to take your skin off?
Like, all of it?
Sometimes I unzip myself and hang me in the wardrobe,
a skin-suit draped macabrely from a hanger,
put my earrings and used-to-be-white teeth in the drawer
and I walk around the room,
this raw human with all this bright pink flesh washing up at the kitchen
sink
and it scares people!
Actually scares them to see what's underneath the costume.
Like, for heavens sake,
cover up your womb woman,
get in your dressing room,
we want you groomed and perfumed.
And sometimes I just want to scream
But this is me!

This Skin I'm In

# Fisheyes

I'm lying on my mat.
Actually, three mats. The hard floor hurts my bones.
What doesn't?
I had tried to move into this pose and got taken down again from left
field.
Trauma with a capital T
whiplashed me,
knocked my tree so hard and so far from centre
it made me enter that room again.
The one I don't think about.
Blink my eyes three times to make it disappear
before the fear
creeps any deeper.

On the outside a sort of dead fish pose
in a yoga class
I suppose.
But underneath fleshy silver scales,
a convulsing child's pose
and
BLINK!
BLINK!
BLINK!

The teacher comes over and does that thing where they softly cup your
head in mother hands
and the frightened dory rubber-bands back to life,
leaking saltwater from bulgy fisheyes
and my body lands
back on the mat
and to my surprise

I am 38.
I am in a yoga studio in East London.
I survived.

This Skin I'm In

# Self Portrait

I look at her,
Who is she?
This woman
That I criticise.
The one with the scars
From picking her spots,
Dimply thighs
And deep brown eyes.

I poke
The ripply contour
Of her belly overhanging,
Judge the anchor shapes
On her chest
Like a mean girl,
Bitchy face scanning.

Her mouth
is slightly wonky,
Her skin is lined
And dry,
And she no longer
Has a gap
Anywhere near
Those thighs.

The teeth need whitening,
The bum tightening,
The hips could do
with more curve.
I stand back,
Take another selfie
That I carefully observe.

I look into those
Lovely eyes

That have bravely
Stared grief in the face.
That have closed
with exhaustion
But never given up,
Wept for the human race.

They've sobbed with joy,
Dilated in shock,
Sparkled
at Christmas lights.
Forget windows
To the soul,
These are skylights.

I look at her mouth,
Her pink little mouth
That has sung lullaby
after lullaby.
Has kissed with heat,
Reassured,
Bravely testified.

I gaze at her hands,
Those chapped,
beautiful hands
That once held
a rattle in glee.
That have reached out,
Helped others up,
Written poetry.

That belly of hers
She hates so much
That grew and birthed
Her boy,

The breasts that fed
Her prem baby
And got her in Playboy.

A slightly different
Pale yellow light
Is streaming
On to her face.
She touches her skin,
Her identical twin,
She is
Grit and grace.

This Skin I'm In

# Too much

The wind makes her skin
feel battered and bruised.
The light assaults her,
electric skin bemused
by air and clothes,
others' words
open-fire blows,
stiletto heels
in her heart,
splattered red fine art
on
white canvas
that said over and over
"She feels too much."

This Skin I'm In

`

# Mockingbird

I hang out of the window,
smoke a fag, smoke a feeling.
My shame floats up in little puffs
sticking to the ceiling.
Then her voice again,
the woman behind the curtain.

**"Keep on running baby.**
**Where you running to?"**

A single tear
softly kisses my cheek.
The mockingbird has stolen my words.
*Anywhere away from here*
*As far away from you,*
I think, looking at my shoes.
My cardigan reeks.
I stub out my cigarette,
chuck it down
onto the street,
stick my fingers in my ears
as she speaks.

**"Don't backchat bitch.**
**I fucking own you.**
**How could you diss me**
**after all I've done for you."**

I get up off the window sill.
Pull up the collar
on my blue check shirt,
cover my hurt.
Wrap my cardi round me
to keep out the chill.

**"Oh my God.**
**Are you actually strutting?**
**Listen to me.**

**You are absolutely nothing.**
**I see you got your hair done.**
**Mate, you're such a joke.**
**Least it hides your face."**
she coos,
and gives my arm a stroke.

But I….

**"Stop. Sit down.**
**Where you going?**
**Shoulders back,**
**fucking glowing."**

I have the audacity to cut my eyes at her.
I know it's unwise.
I sit at my desk,
wild butterflies in my chest
write what I can't verbalise.

**"Come on, baby,**
**it was only a joke.**
**Let's stay together,**
**drink, smoke.**
**Throw that pen and paper in the bin.**
**And what kind of title is 'This skin I'm in?'**

But I want to write a book…

**"I know. But you'll never do it**
**'cos you're scared as fuck.**
**Remember that last rejection,**
**you felt like swinging from a hook!'**

My voice isn't even loud.
It doesn't need to be.
"I'm done with you.
I won't take it anymore.
Who do you think you are
waging your one-woman war?

# This Skin I'm In

You've had your fun,
run the show,
dealt me blow after blow,
monitored my every fucking word,
pinned me in your shadow."

**She falters for a second.**

**"You're acting crazy again,**
**you're on the brink…"**

And you know what I do?
I don't even think.
I hit the mute.
And I watch her throwing her arms around
trying to get my attention,
screaming her silent lungs out
'til she's so tired, she crumples to the kitchen floor like that witch in Oz,
like the puff of hot air she always was.

As I rise from my chair
to go get some air,
I notice a note
in the pocket of my raincoat
which I unfold.
And typed in bold,
her last stranglehold;

**"You'll never leave me,**
**I'm the tie that binds.**
**No one will ever**
**love you like I do.**
**We are the perfect**
**meeting of minds."**

And from my window,
the paper airplane
sails down in the rain.
Thanks shame,
but fuck off all the same.

This Skin I'm In

# Shapeshifter/Shazam

My brain's gone dead
Just lit my vape
In the kitchen
Throwing shapes
Leg it to school
Dodging the cracks
Pavement pounding
Pick up my Prozac
No time to relax
Need to make tracks
30 min rebounding
I know I'm sounding
Manic cos I am
Love a bit of Wham!
Hit Shazam
Like I've done a gram
Just the way I am
Hyped up Van Damme
Shapeshifter
Dolly mixture
Have fun while it lasts
Brain running fast
Cos who knows
Tomorrow's forecast

# Make mine a large

I can't explain
but I need something,
some aliveness,
some big feeling.
To scrape my body
off the floor,
peel my head
off the ceiling.

This Skin I'm In

# Defrost

The edges of my mind
unstitched
nerves switched
off
head lost
plunge me into
iced water
please bitter frost
crackle my bones
bite my skin
bruise my shins
grab me hard
by my heart
and smash me
deep dive
make me feel alive
bones snap back to life
reality drops into focus
mind/body symbiosis
fusing wires together
I gently solder
the severed head to shoulders
thawing out the trauma.
And slowly,
my blood feels warmer.

# Cocktail

A hundred tiny papercuts
sting my grieving skin.
Feels like they're being bathed
in lemons and neat gin.

This Skin I'm In

# The Inbetweeners

I'm under it,
I'm over it,
nails chipped like my heart.
Wish I had
a button on my back
to press the restart.
Down and up,
down and up,
like my Nan's
Singer sewing machine,
stitching the edges
that keep on fraying,
praying to be in between.
Scream in the car
to the beats of The Streets,
turn the radio up.
Muffle the pain,
pick my arm
drain my coffee cup.
Scuff my wheels
on the kerb,
too tired to give a fuck.
Those ones in the middle,
the flatliners
just don't know their luck.

This Skin I'm In

# Wear your Story

My eyebrows look angry
so I must be.
38 year old,
double-spaced eyelids
hooding irises and pupils
whose view have changed
like
my breasts,
rearranged not once but twice,
expertly marked and sliced.
Then this wrist,
brailled in permanent ink
links
arms and hands
who have wounded and caressed,
undressed
the soft belly
covering the part where
(M)other is stencilled on my womb,
the baby's room,
the blank space between
my hips
that never really bloomed,
with capital lettered DON'T TOUCH,
we've felt too much.
You just stay there where we can see you.
We who uttered #UsToo,
who joined forces with time-worn skin
tightly pulled
over ashamed shoulder blades
slightly curved by the decades.
Paper-thin
layers of calligraphy skin
stretch over my thighs
who memorised
stuff they'd rather not have

and skim all the way down past
bruisy shins.
When slowly,
slowly,
those lashes rouse from sleep and weep.
And palm to heart,
I ink a love note,
wrap it around her like a coat,
"You are history.
You are abstract art.
Each body part
torn apart.
This here is your memoir.
If only you knew how exquisite you really are.
I will stitch you back together.
I will mend you."

This Skin I'm In

# Uncuffed

And one day,
as the snow fell soundlessly,
a white space became
to replace
my centre,
pregnant with disgrace for the longest gestation,
the birthplace of untruths
seeded in my youth
as I plucked
the self-fired arrow of blame
from my tender heart
and emptied out the shame
into a litter bin,
gave her a new name,
wiped my tears with kitchen roll,
rough on flimsy skin,
thickening,
and walked out of the shade
uncuffed,
cheeks touched with pale sunlight,
scuffed trainers cast aside,
the swallow gliding
in quiet celebration
who saw me serve time
for this imagined crime.
Wondering why
and how
I ever could have thought me unbeautiful.

# Transplant list

"So, what I'd like to do is take out my organs."
I say,
"Display them on a clean white table,
perhaps label them.

Brain.
You see these ventricles? Yes, they're like minuscule rabbit warrens.
I have crawled through the warrens of my very own brain,
been dragged by my hair through this limbic plane.

Then this here that looks like a rare steak is my actual liver!
A truly remarkable organ.
This has filtered thousands of litres of rage masquerading as peach iced
tea.

And those amber sieves there,
liver's mates, lungs,
winced with every spark up
from my first in the park up on Middledale
to my last just now.

Ah now this one is really special.
You see how it looks like an upside-down pear?
That's where my son grew!
Literally right inside there!
Gosh, wow, I can hardly believe it now but he did.

And oh…
…this one.
What to say about this one?
This nucleus of me
is carved from the Ebony tree
which is valued for its dark heartwood and is classed as extremely
vulnerable.
Heart has navigated the bleakest of spiritual winters
and despite being strewn with splinters
has orchestrated some of the greatest love songs.

## This Skin I'm In

No matter what,
heart will always,
always
love.

And so now they've spoken, been seen, told you where they've been,
it's time to softly wrap them
in layers of tissue

and fold them back into this skin I'm in.

This Skin I'm In

This Skin I'm In

# About blood moon POETRY:

blood moon POETRY is a small indie press and a home for women who write poetry. We feature poetry and illustrations by women from all walks of life, striving to support and amplify marginalised voices in particular. Seeking out new and undiscovered creative women, we specialise in the compilation, editing and publication of print poetry anthologies and pamphlets centred on themes of womanhood. Our bi-annual digital journal also features work from our growing online community of poets, authors and illustrators from all walks of life. We aim to celebrate the diverse beliefs, paths to and complex perspectives on womanhood by showcasing that diversity in our publications.

Connect with us on Instagram @bloodmoonpoetrypress
Find us and subscribe at www.bloodmoonpoetry.com

Printed in Great Britain
by Amazon

68965264R00047